To: Caleb Last

Freedom & Responsibility

What I Learned About Life from Acting, Building Blocks, and Camping

JOSEPH LINDON MCQUIRTER III

Chase your dreams!

From: Grandmother

Copyright © 2023 by Lisa Drew

All rights reserved. No part of this book may be reproduced, distributed, or transmitted in any form or by any means, including photocopying, recording, or other electronic or mechanical methods, without the prior written permission of the publisher, except in the case of brief quotations embodied in critical reviews and certain other noncommercial uses permitted by copyright law.

Disclaimer
The information provided in this book is for general informational purposes only. While the author has made every effort to ensure the accuracy and reliability of the information contained within, neither the publisher nor the author make any representations or warranties of any kind, express or implied, about the completeness, accuracy, reliability, suitability, or availability with respect to the book or the information, products, services, or related graphics contained in the book for any purpose. Any reliance you place on such information is therefore strictly at your own risk. Any views or opinions represented in this book are personal and belong solely to the author, and do not represent those of people, institutions, or organizations that the author may or may not be associated with in a professional or personal capacity unless explicitly stated.

Permissions Requests
Requests to the publisher for permissions should be addressed to:
2227 Old Bridge Rd Woodbridge, VA. 22192 info@redcarpetbusinessexpo.com

Published by Lisa Drew 2227 Old Bridge Rd Woodbridge, VA. 22192
Printed in the U.S.

Foreword

Every mother knows the depth of love and pride she feels for her child, emotions that words often struggle to capture. As I write this foreword for "Freedom & Responsibility: What I Learned About Life from Acting, Building Blocks, and Camping," it's a challenge to convey the whirlwind of emotions – from immense pride to quiet contemplation – that fill my heart.

Holding your child for the first time, you're filled with dreams, wonders, and concerns about their future. Fast forward through the years, and this book has offered me a beautiful lens into the heart and soul of the boy I've raised. It's an intimate dive into his journey, showing not just the milestones but the everyday moments that have molded him.

Acting, building blocks, and camping – to some, a quirky trio, but in our household, they've been gateways to self-discovery. I've seen his eyes light up recounting a scene he's acted in, watched him lose track of time amid a sea of pieces, and listened to enchanting tales from his camping escapades. Each of these activities, in its own way, has added layers to his personality.

Becoming an Eagle Scout isn't merely about badges or ceremonies; it's about character-building, persistence, and understanding one's place in the larger world. Through this phase, I witnessed my son's graceful dance between enjoying his freedoms and shouldering responsibilities.

This book isn't just a peek into scouting adventures or teenage pastimes. It's a heartfelt narrative of a young dreamer, constantly pushing boundaries and discovering himself. As his mother, sharing these intimate tales with you feels both vulnerable and rewarding.

To every person who delves into these pages, I hope you're reminded of the magic of youth, the promise of tomorrow, and the intricate balance that life constantly beckons us to find.

With all my love,

Lisa Drew

Lisa Drew

Table Of Contents

Foreword.. 2
Introduction... 8
    Setting the Stage: The Unexpected Teachers of Life................ 8
    Prologue: Embracing Curiosity..18
    Why Acting, Blocks, and Camping?...22
Chapter 1: The World of Acting.. 26
    1:1 The Mask We Wear: Roles in Life and on Stage............... 29
    1:2 Empathy and Perspective: Walking in Someone Else's Shoes...39
    1:3 Taking Direction: The Importance of Feedback and Growth.. 42
Chapter 2: Lessons from the Spotlight.. 44
    2:1 Embracing Vulnerability: Standing Bare on Stage and in Life..47
    2:2 Improvisation: The Art of Adapting and Thriving in the Unexpected...49
    2:3 Rejections and Callbacks: Dealing with Failures and Celebrating Wins.. 52
Chapter 3: Building with Building Blocks................................... 56
    3:1 Foundation First: The Importance of a Strong Base in Life... 59
    3:2 Creativity and Vision: Imagining and Building Your Dreams.. 62
    3:3 Interlocking Pieces: The Value of Connectivity and Community...64
Chapter 4: Lessons from the Colorful Bricks........................... 66
    4:1 Patience and Persistence: When Your Creation Falls Apart.

4:2 Following Instructions vs. Going Rogue: Balancing Guidance and Intuition............... 70

4:3 The Joy in the Process: Celebrating the Building, Not Just the Finished Product............... 73

Chapter 5: Into the Great Outdoors: Camping........................ 76

5:1 Preparing for the Journey: The Significance of Planning and Preparedness............... 79

5:2 Campfires and Connections: Valuing Community and Shared Stories............... 83

Chapter 6: Lessons Under the Stars............... 86

6:1 Navigating Without Technology: Trusting Instincts and Reading the Natural Signs............... 89

6:2 Minimalism and Resourcefulness: Making Do with What You Have............... 91

6:3 The Quiet Reflection: Insights from Solitude and Disconnection............... 94

Chapter 7: Intersecting Insights............... 98

7:1 Where Acting, Building Blocks, and Camping Collide: Overlapping Lessons from Diverse Experiences............... 101

7:2 Building Your Life's Script: Drawing from Play, Creativity, and Adventure............... 104

7:3 Ensemble Cast: The People Who Shape Our Lives' Narrative............... 107

Chapter 8: Application in Daily Life............... 110

8:1 Strategies to Embrace Play and Creativity in Routine..... 112

8:2 Finding Your Stage, Building Blocks, and Wilderness in Everyday Settings............... 115

Conclusion: Life's Ongoing Lessons............... 120

Embracing New Teachers: Finding Wisdom in Unexpected Places............... 122

The Invitation: Seek, Learn, and Grow from All of Life's

    Experiences... 125
    Parting Thoughts: Your Personal Journey and What Lies Ahead 127
Afterword... **130**
Appendices.. **132**
    Books:... 132
    Workshops:.. 132
    Experiences:.. 133
    Interactive Activities and Challenges for Readers................. 133

Introduction

Setting the Stage: The Unexpected Teachers of Life

Life, in its mysterious and eclectic beauty, is akin to a boundless stage, bustling with actors, playwrights, and unseen directors, all weaving stories in real-time. It's through this stage of existence that unexpected teachers, in the form of experiences and moments, dance into our lives, leaving behind trails of wisdom and echoes of laughter.

Acting: The Art of Expression and Understanding Others
Acting, a passion that lights up my soul, is my teacher of expression and empathy. Slipping into different characters, understanding their motivations, and bringing their stories to life has given me a deeper understanding of the human experience. It's a journey into diverse perspectives, teaching me the power of empathy and the art of effective communication.

My world is colored by a profound passion for acting. It's a journey that's taken me far beyond the stage lights, into a realm where I've learned to navigate the rich and complex world of human emotions. Acting for me isn't just a pursuit of a craft; it's an exploration into the art of understanding and expressing the myriad of feelings that make up the human experience.

A Window into Multiple Realities:

Every character I bring to life is a new adventure, a chance to see the world through a different lens. It's not just about memorizing lines or perfecting expressions; it's about truly embodying another person's life. This immersion gives me the opportunity to understand diverse viewpoints, challenging me to step out of my own experiences and delve into those of others. From the joyous to the troubled, each role becomes a lesson in empathy and understanding.

Building Emotional Depth:

Acting has been my playground for emotional exploration. Each character is a new emotional journey, allowing me to feel and express a range of sentiments that I might not encounter in my everyday life. From the exhilarating highs of love and joy to the somber depths of sorrow and despair, acting has widened my emotional spectrum, making me more attuned to the feelings of others around me. It's taught me to look beneath the surface, to understand the emotions that drive people's actions and words.

The Silent Conversations:

One of the most intriguing aspects of acting is learning the language of non-verbal communication. On stage, a pause, a glance, or a subtle gesture can speak volumes. This nuanced form of expression has made me more observant and sensitive to the unspoken words in real life. Understanding these silent cues has become a vital tool in connecting with others, allowing me to comprehend emotions and thoughts that aren't directly voiced.

Empathy: The Soul of Acting and Life:

Central to acting is the ability to empathize, to genuinely feel and understand the emotions of another character. This skill has transcended the boundaries of the stage and seeped into my everyday interactions. Whether it's relating to a friend's hidden struggles or grasping the nuances of a family member's mood, empathy has allowed me to form deeper, more meaningful relationships.

Acting as a Reflection of Life:

Each role I take on is like a mirror reflecting back aspects of human nature. Through acting, I've learned about love, loss, courage, fear, and the multitude of emotions that define our existence. It's a process that continually teaches me about human psychology, relationships, and the complexities of emotional expression.

My journey through acting has been more than just an artistic endeavor; it's been a path to understanding the intricate tapestry of human emotions. Acting has not only shaped my ability to express and connect but has also given me a deeper insight into the human psyche. In every script, every character, and every performance, I find a piece of life's puzzle, helping me to understand and appreciate the diverse experiences and emotions that weave together the story of humanity. As I continue to explore and grow in this art form, I look forward to the endless lessons and understandings that await in each new role and scene.

Building Blocks: The Blueprint of Creativity and Patience
And then, there are building blocks, my earliest passion. They have been more than just play; they have been my introduction to the world of creativity and patience. Each block is a lesson in paying attention to detail, in understanding that every small part contributes to a larger picture, and that patience can lead to incredible creations. When you have building blocks some people might view them as just a toy, for kids.. To me they are like a treasure trove of life lessons wrapped in colorful plastic. Even though I'm a teenager now I still find solace and inspiration in these blocks. They have taught

me much about being creative, patient and facing challenges head on.

Creativity; Unleashing Magic with Blocks

Every time I open a box of building blocks it feels like entering a world where endless possibilities exist. Each block presents an opportunity to construct something unique. Whether I'm building a castle or a quirky little vehicle these blocks encourage me to think outside the box and explore ideas. They have shown me that creativity goes beyond creating art; it involves perceiving the world from angles and having the courage to bring imaginative concepts to life.

Patience; One Block at a Time

Creating something doesn't happen instantly – it requires patience and perseverance one block, at a time. There are moments when my initial attempts don't succeed, not on the second try.
These building blocks have been teachers, for me reminding me that achieving the results requires time and effort. It's about adding one

piece at a time, making adjustments along the way and not losing hope even if it takes many attempts to get it right.

Solving Problems; Thinking Beyond the Blocks)

Building blocks have this way of teaching problem solving skills. I've encountered block dilemmas" where what I'm trying to construct doesn't seem to come as planned. These moments feel like fun and interactive puzzles. They have taught me to explore approaches, think quickly on my feet and persist until I discover a solution that works perfectly.

Collaboration; Constructing Together

Some of my memories with building blocks involve collaborating with friends or family members. When we work together on a construction project it's not just about what we're creating; it's about valuing each other's ideas, compromising when needed and enjoying the process as a team. This experience has shown me the power of collaboration and how our combined efforts can lead to something remarkable.

Although my collection of building blocks may appear like child's play at glance it has actually provided me with lessons in essential life skills.

These building blocks have influenced my perspective on creativity, patience, problem solving and collaborating with others. They serve as a reminder that valuable lessons can often come from the things. As I continue to mature and encounter challenges, in life I will always carry with me the teachings of my vibrant building blocks; approach tasks gradually embrace creative thinking and don't hesitate to start anew if necessary.

Camping: The Teacher of Resilience and Adaptability

Under the canvas of stars, camping has taught me resilience. Nature, in its untamed beauty, brings unforeseen challenges – sudden storms, difficult terrains, and the need to coexist with the wild. These experiences have shaped my ability to adapt, to find solutions in the face of scarcity, and to appreciate the simplicity of life away from the chaos of the modern world.

Camping is more than a weekend pastime for me; it's like attending a school beneath the twinkling stars. I discovered that my wilderness adventures have taught me life lessons in resilience and adaptability. In the embrace of nature I've learned how to thrive in situations that push me out of my comfort zone.

Resilience; Weathering Life's Storms

Camping has brought me face to face with challenges ranging from thunderstorms to demanding trails. These experiences have instilled resilience within me. Setting up a tent amidst winds, keeping the fire burning during rainfall or finding my way when the trail becomes unclear have all demonstrated that I possess the capability to overcome obstacles. It's not about enduring circumstances; it's about learning to find solutions and carrying on even when things don't unfold as planned.

Adaptability; Natures Unpredictable Lessons

When it comes to the outdoors one thing you can always count on is that nothing goes precisely according to plan. I've learned how to adapt whether it means altering routes, adjusting plans due to inclement weather or discovering cooking methods when our camp stove fails. These moments of problem solving are not just about thinking; they also involve being open minded and adaptable when faced with changes.

Independence and Self Reliance

Camping has taught me valuable lessons in self reliance. When you're out in the wilderness you have to depend on your skills and resources. Setting up camp, cooking meals over a fire and navigating through nature – these experiences have shown me that I can be independent and confident in my abilities. It's empowering for any teenager to realize that they can take care of themselves and those around them.

Connecting with the Natural World

Beyond the skills and challenges camping has deeply connected me with nature. It's one thing to read about the environment. Living in it only for a weekend is an entirely different experience. I've developed an appreciation for the beauty of the world while also understanding the importance of preserving it.

Each camping trip has been a journey towards building resilience and adaptability. These are skills that I know will benefit me not during camping but in all aspects of life.

Camping has been an experience, for me, teaching me the value of embracing challenges, being resourceful and appreciating the beauty of nature. With every adventure I eagerly anticipate the valuable lessons that await me.

In these activities, I find the essence of life's teachings – resilience, responsibility, empathy, creativity, and patience. They are more than pastimes; they are the stages where I learn, grow, and prepare for the grand performance of life. Each has set the stage for me to embrace life's challenges and triumphs, making me realize that sometimes, the best teachers are the experiences we encounter in our passions.

Prologue: Embracing Curiosity

From the moment we open our eyes to the world, we're imbued with an innate curiosity, a spark propelling us to explore, wonder, and learn. The whispering winds, the murmuring streams, every rustle in the leaves become the unseen mentors whispering lessons of flow, resilience, and adaptation.

Life's Ensemble: The Roles We Play

We all adorn different masks, playing varying roles, becoming the son, the friend, the mentor, the student. It's through these multitudes of interactions that we grasp the essence of empathy, understand the nuances of relationships, and appreciate the symphony of interconnected lives. The shifting roles teach us flexibility, understanding, and the beauty of seeing the world through different lenses.

The Unseen Directors: Embracing the Unplanned

Our paths are not always drafted by us. Sometimes, the unseen directors of life place us in unanticipated scenes, scripting unchosen narratives. It's these unplanned acts that teach us the elegance of letting go, the strength in vulnerability, and the power in acceptance. The spontaneity of life encourages us to dance in the rhythm of uncertainty and find harmony in chaos.

Acting and Reacting: The Art of Response

The stage of life is a dynamic exchange of actions and reactions, of words spoken and unspoken. How we respond to the dialogues of life, to the unscripted challenges, determines the essence of our character and the depth of our wisdom. It's in the pauses, the reflections, the quiet moments that we learn the value of thoughtful response over hasty reaction, the impact of kindness over judgment.

The Final Bow: Gratitude for Every Act

As the curtains close on varied acts of our lives, and as we bow in front of the silent audience of stars, we learn the profoundness of gratitude. Gratitude for the challenges that shaped us, for the laughter that healed us, and for the moments that defined us. The essence of being thankful for every act, every interaction, elevates our existence, enriching our soul with peace and contentment.

Encore: Continuous Learning

Even when the lights dim and the audience leaves, our learning never ceases. Every echo in the empty hall, every lingering note teaches us the importance of continuous growth, of seeking knowledge, and of valuing every experience. The unending journey of learning teaches us humility, the joy in discovery, and the bliss in evolving.

Final Thoughts: A Symphony of Lessons

In the grand, intricate play of life, every moment is a teacher, every experience a lesson. We're eternal students, learning the dance of existence, understanding the music of the cosmos, and growing in the garden of wisdom. So, let's step onto the stage of life with open hearts, embrace the unexpected teachers with open arms, and dance in the rhythm of continuous learning, creating a symphony of insights, a ballad of wisdom.

Remember, life's a stage brimming with countless acts, unexpected directors, and unseen teachers. The beauty lies in embracing every moment, learning every lesson, and cherishing every act. So, let's set the stage, embrace the teachers, and dance in the everlasting rhythm of life!

Why Acting, Blocks, and Camping?

Have you ever sat down and reminisced about childhood memories or stories, only to realize that the most unexpected activities gave you the profoundest insights? That's the magic of life. The seemingly unrelated can harbor the deepest of life's wisdom. So, why Acting, Building Blocks, and Camping? Let's break it down, scene by scene, brick by brick, campfire by campfire.

Acting: The Reflective Mirror

Acting isn't just about reciting lines or mimicking emotions. It's an exploration into the deep waters of human experiences. It's about understanding a character, feeling their emotions, and embracing their flaws. Through acting, we're taught empathy – the ability to feel and understand emotions that aren't inherently our own. It's a journey of introspection and perspective. Life, like a script, unfolds in acts, each scene bringing with it new emotions, challenges, and characters. By embracing the essence of acting, we learn to navigate life's play, adapting to its unpredictable scripts, and empathizing with its myriad characters.

Building Blocks: Building Life, Brick by Brick

Remember that excitement of opening a new box of building blocks? The scattered bricks, waiting to become something amazing? That's life for you! We're given bricks – experiences, memories, lessons, challenges, and joys. Each brick fits somewhere, sometimes seamlessly, sometimes requiring a bit of pressure. Building Blocks teach us patience and the art of creation. They remind us that even if something falls apart, we can always build again, perhaps even better this time. Just like life, where every experience, every moment, is a building block leading to the grand design of our destiny.

Camping: The Call of the Wilderness

Away from the screens, the concrete jungles, the hustle and bustle, camping takes us back to our roots. It's an embrace of the raw, the wild, the untamed. Amidst the chirping of crickets, the rustling of leaves, and the crackling of campfires, we find profound silence. A silence that allows introspection. Camping teaches us resilience – the art of surviving, even thriving, with minimal resources. It reminds us of the beauty of simplicity, the value of disconnecting to truly connect, and the importance of being present. Every campsite, every trail, every dawn and dusk brings with it lessons of perseverance, adaptability, and the pure, unadulterated joy of being alive.

Acting, Building Blocks, and Camping might seem like an odd trio at first glance. Yet, if you look a little closer, dig a little deeper, you'll find that they're not just hobbies or pastimes. They're profound teachers, each bringing forth lessons that shape our character, guide our journey, and enrich our soul. Life, in all its grandeur, is a combination of scripts, building blocks, and adventures. So, let's take a cue from these unexpected teachers and embrace the wisdom they offer, navigating life with empathy, creativity, and the spirit of adventure.

Chapter 1: The World of Acting

When we think of acting, we often envision bright lights, intricate costumes, applause, and, of course, Oscar speeches. But beneath the glitz and glam, the world of acting is a treasure trove of life lessons waiting to be discovered.

1. A Step into Another's Shoes

At its core, acting is about stepping into another's shoes, understanding their motivations, fears, dreams, and desires. It's a deep dive into the human psyche and emotions. This skill isn't just for the stage; it's crucial in real life too. Whether it's understanding a colleague's perspective at work or empathizing with a friend's struggles, the practice of seeing the world through another's eyes can lead to deeper connections and a more compassionate approach to life.

2. Embrace Vulnerability

Actors, in the pursuit of authenticity, often lay their emotions bare for audiences to see. It's about embracing vulnerability, shedding masks, and being genuine. In our own lives, while it's challenging, showing our true selves, with all our imperfections, can lead to genuine relationships and a true sense of self-worth.

3. The Art of Adaptability

On stage or on set, things don't always go as planned. A co-actor might forget a line, or a prop could malfunction. Great actors improvise. Life too is unpredictable. Those who can think on their feet, adapting to life's unexpected turns, are often the ones who find success and contentment.

4. The Value of Persistence

Rejections are a part and parcel of an actor's life. Yet, they persist, attending audition after audition, honing their craft, believing in their passion. Similarly, in life, we face setbacks and failures. But the road to success, contentment, and personal growth is paved with persistence, grit, and a never-give-up attitude.

5. The Power of Observation

Actors are keen observers. They pick up quirks, mannerisms, and nuances which they infuse into their characters, making them come alive. Observing the world around us, being in the moment, can lead to rich experiences, insights, and a deeper appreciation of life's tapestry.

In the Spotlight:

While acting might seem like a world apart, it's deeply intertwined with the essence of being human. The highs and lows, the joys and challenges, the tears and laughter; actors bring these to the stage and screen, reminding us of our shared human experience. Delving into the world of acting is not just about the drama and the accolades, but about understanding life's profound truths. So, whether you're an avid theater-goer, an amateur actor, or just someone navigating the grand stage of life, there's a lot to learn from the world of acting. And who knows? You might just find your own spotlight along the way.

1:1 The Mask We Wear: Roles in Life and on Stage

At some point in our lives, we've all donned a mask, both literally and metaphorically. On Halloween, we become superheroes or villains, and in theater, an actor becomes the character they portray. But away from the spotlight and festivities, we wear other masks daily, often without even realizing it.

1. The Pressure to Conform

From a young age, society often expects us to fit into neat little boxes. Be the diligent student, the responsible sibling, or the ambitious employee. These roles come with masks — the facade we put up to meet those expectations. It's like a performance on the world's stage, one where we sometimes forget our authentic selves in favor of the character we think we should play.

In a world teeming with societal norms and expectations, the pressure to conform can feel like a relentless tide, pushing us towards a preordained mold. From the clothes we wear to the careers we choose, the invisible currents of conformity are omnipresent, subtly influencing our decisions and shaping our identities. As individuals, especially in the formative years of youth, navigating these currents while trying to hold onto our unique selves can be a daunting challenge.

The Social Mirror: Reflecting Expectations

Society often acts like a mirror, reflecting back a set of standards and expectations. These can range from simple fashion choices to deeper life decisions like academic and career paths. The desire to fit in, to be accepted, and the fear of being labeled as 'different' can lead many of us to alter our true selves, adopting personas and choices that align more with societal norms than with our genuine preferences and aspirations.

Conformity in Youth: The Crossroads of Identity

For young people, this pressure can be particularly intense. High school halls and college campuses are rife with unspoken rules about how to act, dress, and even think. The quest to find one's identity is often entangled with the need to belong to a group, leading many youths to suppress their uniqueness in favor of a more socially acceptable persona. This struggle can lead to internal conflicts, as the desire for individuality clashes with the comfort of conformity.

The Cost of Conformity: Losing Oneself

One of the most significant dangers of conforming is the loss of individuality. Constantly molding ourselves to fit into societal expectations can lead to a loss of personal identity and values. It can stifle creativity, discourage original thought, and even affect mental health, as the pressure to maintain a facade can be exhausting and unfulfilling.

Breaking Free: The Courage to Be Yourself

Finding the courage to break free from the shackles of conformity requires self-awareness and confidence. It's about embracing one's uniqueness, accepting that being different is not only okay but valuable. It involves making choices that align with one's true self, even if they go against the grain of societal norms. This path is not easy, as it often comes with the risk of social ostracization, but the reward is a life lived authentically and freely.

The pressure to conform is an undeniable part of society, but it doesn't have to dictate our lives. By recognizing and understanding these pressures, we can make conscious decisions that honor our true selves. It's a journey of balancing societal expectations with personal authenticity, a journey that ultimately leads to a more fulfilling and genuine existence. In the grand tapestry of life, each individual thread of nonconformity adds color and richness, contributing to a more diverse and vibrant whole.

2. Fear of Judgment

Just as an actor fears a critic's review, we fear judgment from peers, family, or even strangers. This fear can push us to hide our true selves, adopting a mask that's more 'acceptable' or 'normal'. Over time, constantly wearing this mask can be exhausting and can drift us away from our true nature.

The fear of being judged has an impact on aspects of our lives. It affects how we perceive ourselves, how we interact with our family and friends and even the choices we make. This fear arises from sources, such as the expectations our parents have for us, the pressure from our peers and even our own inner critic. It often holds us back from expressing ourselves. Pushes us towards paths that may not align with our genuine desires and aspirations.

Parental Judgment; Striking a Balance between Expectations and Authenticity

Many of us experience judgment as one of the forms of assessment in our lives. Parents, with intentions, set expectations based on their beliefs, experiences and hopes for us. However these expectations can sometimes become burdensome when they clash with our dreams and sense of identity. The desire to please our parents or meet their standards can overshadow our ambitions resulting in a life focused more on meeting expectations than exploring who we truly are.

Peer Judgment; The Pressure to Conform

During the young adult years in particular peer judgment holds great influence, over shaping who we are and the choices we make. The pressure to fit in and be accepted by our circles often leads us to conform, at the expense of suppressing our individuality. This can mean changing how we look, what we're interested in and how we behave to match the expectations of our peers. Unfortunately this can result in losing a sense of authenticity and personal fulfillment.

Dealing with Self Criticism; Our Inner Judge

One of the forms of judgment comes from within ourselves. Our inner critic can be relentless questioning our choices, abilities and self worth. This self judgment often mirrors the judgments we fear or have experienced. It can significantly hinder our self confidence and acceptance of who we're keeping us trapped in doubt and preventing us from embracing our identity.

Navigating the Journey to Self Acceptance

Overcoming the fear of judgment—whether its from our parents, friends or even ourselves—is crucial for growth and happiness. It involves developing a sense of self rooted in our values and aspirations. Key steps on this journey include embracing what makes us unique, understanding that our worth isn't dependent on others approval and learning to trust our intuition while also being open to feedback.

It's about finding a balance between considering input from others while staying true, to ourselves and forging our own path.

Overcoming the fear of judgment is a journey that leads us to discover ourselves and live authentically. It takes bravery to break free from the expectations of others and embrace who we really are. As we navigate the pressures of peer expectations as well as our own self doubts we learn to cherish our unique identity and make choices that truly resonate with our inner being. By confronting and surpassing the fear of being judged by others we open ourselves up to a life that's not more genuine but also filled with fulfillment and happiness.

3. Breaking Free from the Mask

In theater, when the curtain falls, actors shed their characters and return to their real selves. They understand the distinction between the role and their identity. In life, it's crucial to realize that the roles we play — whether it's a parent, partner, employee, or friend — are just aspects of our multifaceted selves. They don't define our entire identity. Embracing this understanding can be liberating, allowing us to live authentically.

Ever felt like you're putting on a show, playing a part just to fit in or be liked? I've been there, wearing a metaphorical mask to meet others' expectations or to hide what I really felt or thought. It's like playing a character in your own life story, and let me tell you, it's exhausting. But here's what I've learned on my journey to drop the act and embrace who I really am.

The Masks We Choose

We all wear masks at some point – maybe it's pretending to be more confident than we feel, or hiding our true opinions to avoid conflict. My mask was the 'always happy, always agreeable' one. It was easier to smile and nod than to show my real feelings or disagree.

But constantly playing it safe and hiding behind a facade felt like I was betraying my true self.

The Cost of Keeping Up Appearances

Keeping up this charade was draining. It's like constantly being on stage, never letting your guard down. I realized I was losing touch with who I was – my passions, my beliefs, even my sense of humor. I was so busy trying to be what I thought others wanted that I started to feel isolated, like I was losing my identity.

The Turning Point: Choosing Authenticity

Things started to change when I hit a point where I just couldn't keep up the act anymore. It was scary to think about dropping the mask – what if people didn't like the real me? But I was tired of feeling fake. I decided it was time to be honest about my feelings and opinions, even if it meant risking disapproval.

Embracing Vulnerability: The Real Me

Letting people see the real me was terrifying but also liberating. I started to express my true thoughts, to disagree, to show my quirks, and to embrace my flaws. Sure, not everyone liked it, but being vulnerable opened the door to more genuine relationships. It felt like a weight had been lifted – I was no longer carrying the burden of pretense.

Walking the Path of Honesty

Choosing authenticity is an ongoing journey. It's not about being perfect; it's about being real. For me, it's a daily choice to be honest with myself and others, to stand by my values, and to accept that not everyone will like or agree with me – and that's okay. It's a path that requires courage and self-compassion, but it's worth every step. Ditching the disguise and living authentically has been one of the most challenging yet rewarding changes in my life. It's brought me a sense of freedom and self-respect I never had before. While the fear of judgment and rejection is still there, it no longer controls me. I've learned that the most fulfilling connections and experiences come when you have the courage to be your true self. And trust me, it's a lot more fun being unapologetically you.

4. The Strength in Vulnerability

Actors often tap into their own experiences and vulnerabilities to bring depth to their roles. Similarly, there's power in showing our vulnerabilities in real life. It's when we let our guard down, remove the mask, and show our genuine emotions that we forge deeper connections and truly understand ourselves.

5. Every Mask Has a Story

Every role an actor plays comes with its backstory, its joys, and its challenges. In our lives, every mask we wear has its own story, too.

Instead of judging ourselves or others based on the mask, delving deeper to understand the story behind it can lead to empathy, acceptance, and a richer human experience.

6. Behind the Mask

Life is a complex tapestry of experiences and roles, filled with moments that shape who we are. While it's natural to wear masks in certain situations, it's essential to recognize when the mask becomes a barrier to our true selves. By reflecting on our roles, both on the stage of life and in the theater, we can navigate our journey with authenticity, compassion, and depth, always remembering that beneath every mask lies a human heart, full of stories, dreams, and infinite potential.

1:2 Empathy and Perspective: Walking in Someone Else's Shoes

Have you ever tried on someone else's shoes? Maybe they were too tight, too loose, or just felt plain odd. This unfamiliarity is often how we feel when we try to understand someone else's perspective without empathy. But just as breaking in a new pair of shoes can be rewarding, so can the journey of truly understanding someone else.

1. The Two-Step Dance of Understanding

Empathy isn't just about feeling sorry for someone. It's about genuinely understanding their emotions, challenges, and viewpoint. Think of it as a dance - the first step is to listen, truly and deeply. The second, to reflect and respond without judgment. This dance, when practiced regularly, transforms mere interactions into genuine connections.

2. Different Shoes, Different Views

Just as everyone has their favorite pair of shoes, each individual views the world through their unique lens, molded by experiences, upbringing, and beliefs. By recognizing these differences, we begin to appreciate the richness of human diversity and understand that there isn't always a single 'right' view.

3. Shoes Can Be Deceptive

From the outside, stilettos might look glamorous, but only the wearer knows the pinches and aches. Similarly, someone's life might seem perfect from the outside, but we seldom see their struggles, fears, or challenges. By realizing that appearances can be deceptive, we learn to approach others with compassion and openness.

4. Walking Barefoot: Our Shared Humanity

While it's essential to recognize and appreciate our differences, it's equally important to understand what unites us. At our core, irrespective of the shoes we wear, we all seek love, acceptance, and purpose. By focusing on these shared desires, we find common ground and create a foundation for genuine empathy.

5. The Journey Ahead

Empathy isn't a destination; it's a continuous journey. The world evolves, people change, and new shoes get added to our collection. By regularly trying to walk in them, by regularly engaging with others and seeking to understand their perspectives, we not only enrich our own lives but also make the world a little more compassionate, one step at a time.

In Another's Footsteps:

Empathy is more than a buzzword or a fleeting emotion. It's the bridge that connects us, the balm that heals misunderstandings, and the light that illuminates the dark corners of human experiences. By choosing to walk in someone else's shoes, even just for a short while, we open doors to new worlds, new friendships, and deeper understanding. The journey might be uncomfortable at times, but the vistas of human connection it unveils make every step worth it. So, lace up, step out, and let's embark on this journey of shared humanity together.

1:3 Taking Direction: The Importance of Feedback and Growth

Ever been lost and asked a stranger for directions? It's a humbling experience, realizing you don't have all the answers. In life, as on the acting stage, we often find ourselves in need of guidance. And that's where feedback - our life's director - steps in.

1. Egos Aside, Ears Open

It's easy to think we've got it all figured out. But, like an actor immersed in their role, we might miss the broader picture. Feedback is our reality check. It's not about bruising egos, but about refining our performance, whether on stage or in the grand theater of life.

2. The Script and Improv of Life

While life doesn't come with a script, feedback provides the critical cues. Sometimes, it's an affirmation that you're on the right track. Other times, it's a nudge to try a different approach. Like a director suggesting a change in tone or emotion, feedback guides us to adapt and evolve.

3. Building Resilience, Scene by Scene

Not all feedback is easy to swallow. Some might sting, like a critic's harsh review. But each piece, positive or not-so-great, is an opportunity to grow. By learning to accept, reflect upon, and act on feedback, we build resilience and equip ourselves to face life's varied scenes with grace.

4. The Ensemble Cast of Feedback

Think of life as a play with an ensemble cast. Every person - be it a colleague, friend, or family member - offers a unique perspective, a different angle to our story. Valuing their feedback is about respecting their view and understanding that growth is a collective endeavor.

5. Curtain Call: Embracing Growth

As the curtain falls, an actor knows the value of the director's insights, the feedback from fellow actors, and even the audience's reaction. Similarly, as we navigate life's acts, embracing feedback and direction allows us to continually refine our role, ensuring our life's performance is one for the ages.

Director's Note:

Life isn't a solo performance. It's a collaborative masterpiece, shaped by interactions, experiences, and feedback. Every piece of guidance, every bit of direction, is a stepping stone to growth. So, the next time life - or someone in it - offers you feedback, take a moment. Listen. Reflect. And then act. Because in the grand play of life, feedback isn't just direction; it's an invitation to shine brighter.

Chapter 2: Lessons from the Spotlight

Ever been center stage, feeling the heat of the lights, hearing the hushed whispers of the audience? The spotlight - it's not just about being seen but also about what you learn while you're in it. Acting might seem like it's all about applause and accolades, but the lessons learned in the heart of the limelight? They resonate far beyond the confines of any theater.

1. Embrace the Jitters

Let's face it: being in the spotlight can be nerve-wracking. Those butterflies in your stomach? They're universal. Whether presenting a project, speaking up in a meeting, or even trying something new, the jitters signify that you care. Embrace them. They're a testament to your passion.

2. Imperfection is Gold

You forgot a line, missed a cue, or maybe your voice cracked a bit. It happens. In the spotlight, mistakes become glaringly apparent. But they're also moments of genuine humanity. Life, like acting, isn't about perfection; it's about authenticity, raw emotion, and the beauty in our shared imperfections.

3. Being Seen vs. Being True

There's a difference between just standing in the spotlight and truly owning it. It's not about basking in attention, but about being genuine, making connections, and touching hearts. Whether it's in acting or life, remember: it's not always about being seen but about being true.

4. The Ebb and Flow of Recognition

Some performances will earn you standing ovations; others might be met with silence. The same goes for life's endeavors. Recognition is rewarding, but its absence doesn't negate your worth or efforts. The spotlight teaches you to value the journey, not just the applause.

5. Vulnerability is Strength

Putting yourself out there, in full view, is no small feat. It takes guts. It requires you to be vulnerable. And through that vulnerability, in that spotlight, you find strength. Acting teaches that opening up, being raw and real, is where the magic truly happens.

Encore Thoughts:

The theater, with its dazzling lights and shadowed corners, is much like life. In the spotlight, we discover ourselves, our strengths, and even our shortcomings. We learn to be brave, to be real, and to cherish each moment - applause or none. Remember, it's not just about how long you're in the light, but what you do while you're in it. So, the next time life thrusts you center stage, dance, sing, or simply speak your truth. Every spotlight moment is a lesson waiting to unfold.

2:1 Embracing Vulnerability: Standing Bare on Stage and in Life

You ever had that dream? You know the one. You're suddenly thrust onto a stage, under a harsh, unforgiving spotlight, and - the kicker - you're completely and utterly naked. Panic sets in, the heart races, and you're frantically searching for a quick exit. But what if, instead of fleeing, you owned that moment? Embraced it? This, my friend, is the power of vulnerability.

1. The Paradox of Exposure

It's a weird twist of fate: our most exposed, vulnerable moments often become our most empowering. On stage, an actor's most raw, unplugged performances tend to be the most memorable. In life, our scars, stories, and stumbles, when shared, become sources of connection and strength.

2. The Mask and the Face Beneath

We all wear masks. It's easier to play a character in life, hiding behind what's comfortable and safe. But here's the real deal: The face beneath, with its laugh lines, tears, and genuine expressions? That's where real connection happens. Shedding the mask, on stage and in life, is terrifying but oh-so liberating.

3. Ditching the Script

Sometimes, the most profound moments on stage aren't scripted. They're unplanned, unguarded moments of pure emotion. Life's like that too. Ditching the script, being open to change, and letting yourself feel? It's scary but can lead to the most transformative experiences.

4. The Standing Ovation of Authenticity

Actors will tell you: there's a distinct difference in the applause received for a well-acted performance and the roar of an audience moved by raw, unfiltered emotion. Similarly, in life, the praise we get for being our true selves? It's on a different level. Authenticity attracts authenticity.

5. Finding Courage in the Quiver

Embracing vulnerability isn't about not being scared. It's about feeling that fear, that quiver in your voice, that tremble in your knees, and going ahead anyway. Whether it's confessing a feeling, trying something new, or simply being open about your story - vulnerability is the bridge to deeper connections.

Heart-to-Heart Moment:

Vulnerability? It's not a sign of weakness, but a badge of courage. Standing bare, metaphorically (or literally, in that recurring dream), allows us to embrace the full spectrum of human emotions. It's about realizing that our soft spots, our tender underbellies, are what make us human. And in that humanity, when we dare to be open, to be raw, to be real - that's when we truly come alive. So next time you feel vulnerable, remember: it's your soul's way of asking you to be brave, to be genuine, and most importantly, to be you.

2:2 Improvisation: The Art of Adapting and Thriving in the Unexpected

Ever been caught off-guard? Someone throws you a curveball, and you're left stuttering, trying to find the right response. Or perhaps, you've been in a situation where plans went haywire, and you had to think on your feet. Welcome to the world of improvisation—a realm where spontaneity reigns and adaptability is king.

1. Life's Unscripted Moments

Real talk: Life rarely goes according to plan. Just when you think you've got things under control, BAM! An unexpected twist. But it's in these unscripted moments that we discover our true grit and creativity.

2. The "Yes, And..." Principle

In improv, there's this golden rule: always agree, then add to it. It's about building on ideas, not shutting them down. Imagine if we applied this to life? Embracing opportunities, adding our unique twist, and just...going with the flow.

3. Mistakes: The Unexpected Stepping Stones

In improv, there's no such thing as a 'mistake.' A forgotten line or a surprise turn can lead to the funniest, most memorable moments. Life's like that too. Those hiccups? They often pave the way for growth, learning, and belly laughs.

4. Embracing the Unknown with Gusto

The thrill of improv? The unknown. Every scene is a blank canvas, every interaction an opportunity. Embracing the unexpected with gusto, whether on stage or in life, makes for unforgettable adventures.

5. Listening, The Heart of Improv

Improv isn't just about quick wit; it's about deep, active listening. It's tuning into your partners, catching nuances, and reacting genuinely. In life, truly listening can transform relationships, open doors, and heal wounds.

Real Talk Moment:

Life is one giant improv session. There's no script, no pre-determined outcome. Just a series of moments where we get to choose our response. We can resist the unexpected, or we can roll with it, adapt, and create something beautiful on the fly. So the next time life throws you off script, remember: you've got this. Embrace the art of improvisation. Laugh at the missteps, celebrate the wins, and most importantly, enjoy the ride. It's all part of the glorious, messy performance of life. And guess what? You're nailing it.

2:3 Rejections and Callbacks: Dealing with Failures and Celebrating Wins

"Sorry, we've chosen to go with someone else." Those words sting, don't they? Whether it's from a casting director, a potential employer, or even a love interest, rejection can feel like a slap in the face. It's like preparing for weeks, practicing your lines, getting into character, and then being told, "Not quite right." It's a tough pill to swallow.

But let's flip the script, shall we?

1. The Character Building of 'No'
You see, every "no" you encounter is merely a redirection, not a reflection of your worth. Think about it. Were you ever so glad a particular role went to someone else because the next one that came along was just perfect for you? Similarly, life's rejections often pave the way for better-suited opportunities.

2. Callbacks: The Sweet Affirmation
Ah, the thrill of a callback! It's the universe saying, "Hey, good job! Let's see that again." But remember, just because you get a callback

doesn't mean you've landed the part. It's an invitation to push harder, refine your act, and give it another shot.

3. The Ensemble Cast of Life
You can't play every role. Sometimes, it's not your time to be the lead. And that's okay. Supporting roles often hold the story together. They're pivotal, even if they aren't in every scene. In life, it's essential to understand when to step forward and when to support others.

4. Celebrate Every Win, No Matter How Small
A standing ovation is fantastic, but so is the joy of nailing a challenging scene or getting a tough line right. Celebrate the callbacks, the landed roles, but also cherish the growth from the missed opportunities.

5. Remember: It's a Long Play, Not a One-Act Show
Your life, much like your acting career, is extensive and varied. There will be flops, standing ovations, harsh critics, and raving fans. It's all part of the grand play of life. Embrace each act, learn from the challenges, and always be ready for the next scene.

Curtain Close:

So, next time that rejection email lands in your inbox or you hear yet another "no," remember this: You're still in the running. The play isn't over. Take a breather, review your lines, refine your moves, and get ready to steal the show in the next act. Your standing ovation is just around the corner. Just keep auditioning.

Chapter 3: Building with Building Blocks

Remember the rush of excitement as a kid, pouring out that box of building blocks and seeing a scattered mess of possibilities? The multicolored blocks, the challenges of constructing something worthy, the inevitable foot pain from stepping on a rogue piece—ah, the memories! But as we step back into those plastic-bricked memories, there's more to glean than just nostalgic joy.

1. **Starting Block by Block**

Every grand building block castle starts with a single block. It's a testament to how small beginnings can lead to massive outcomes. Got a dream? Start small, lay your foundation block, and then keep adding to it. Before you know it, you'll be looking at your own masterpiece.

2. **Embrace the Blueprint (But Don't Be Bound by It)**

Those block sets come with manuals, guiding our young (and not-so-young) hands in creating something specific. Life, too, has its 'manuals'—societal expectations, family pressures, self-imposed benchmarks. But sometimes, the most magnificent creations come when we diverge a bit from the instructions.

3. **The Beauty of Interconnection**

One building piece, on its own, is pretty unremarkable. But connect it with others, and it becomes part of something much bigger. It's a reminder of our interconnected lives, how forming bonds and fostering relationships can lead to something truly remarkable.

4. Reconstruction and Adaptation

Ever built a spaceship, only for it to crash and break apart? Heartbreaking, right? But also an opportunity—to rebuild, often into something even better. It's life's way of saying, "Mistakes happen, plans falter, but there's always a chance to start anew, and maybe create something even more awesome."

5. Celebrating Individuality in Unity

Building Blocks come in various shapes, sizes, and colors. Each piece, unique in its design, contributes to the bigger picture. Similarly, our diverse backgrounds, experiences, and ideas make our collective human experience rich and vibrant.

A Building Block Lover's Reflection:

Those tiny blocks taught us so much more than just building techniques. They were early life lessons in patience, creativity, resilience, and the joy of creation. As adults, we might not spill building blocks across the floor as often, but the lessons they ingrained remain. In every challenge, every new endeavor, remember those little blocks and the vast worlds they built. In life, as in blocks, all you need is a bit of creativity and the persistence to keep building.

3:1 Foundation First: The Importance of a Strong Base in Life

"Bro, have you ever tried building that massive Star Destroyer without following the steps or even just winging it? Spoiler: It's a one-way ticket to Frustration Town."

1. The Groundwork of Dreams

We all have towering dreams, much like that 4,784-piece block set. But just as you wouldn't start placing random bricks together, you can't rush your life goals. Everything significant starts with a solid foundation. Whether it's education, a career, relationships, or personal growth—having a strong base ensures that whatever you build atop remains steady.

2. The Underappreciated Base Plate

Man, do you remember those flat building blocks pieces we used to get? They seemed kind of dull compared to the flashy bricks, right? But without them, our creations would lack stability. Similarly, in life, it's the mundane, daily routines and the values we adhere to that act as our base plate, holding everything together.

3. Patience in Laying the First Layer

It's tempting to want to see the end result quickly. But laying down the first bricks—whether it's the basics of a skill, the initial phases of a relationship, or the first steps into adulting—it's crucial to be patient and meticulous. Remember, the sturdiest structures took time to build.

4. When The Foundation Is Wobbly

Ever been halfway through a blocks project and realized you missed a brick way down at the beginning? It sucks! Sometimes, in life, we realize our foundation has gaps. It's okay to deconstruct and rebuild. In fact, it's necessary. Patch those holes, re-evaluate, and continue building.

5. Using the Right Pieces for the Base

Just as you wouldn't use a window pane as a base brick in your tower, in life, it's essential to discern what elements form your foundation. Surround yourself with the right people, cultivate the right habits, and invest in long-lasting materials (like knowledge, love, and health).

Building Thoughts:

Whether you're into building blocks or not, the lesson remains—your life's structure will only be as robust as its foundation. So, before you aim for the stars, make sure you're firmly rooted on the ground. And hey, while you're at it, maybe dig out those old block sets. Building them can be a brilliant (and fun) reminder of life's foundational truths.

3:2 Creativity and Vision: Imagining and Building Your Dreams

"Man, do you remember the sheer joy of dumping a box of building blocks on the floor? The chaos of colorful pieces, waiting to be turned into something epic? That's kinda how our dreams work."

1. The Blank Canvas of Dreams

Each one of us has a scattered pile of potential, much like those random block pieces. They're vibrant, diverse, and waiting for imagination to breathe life into them. Your dreams, no matter how wild or unconventional, are valid and are your own blank canvas.

2. There's No 'Wrong' in Creative Building

Did you ever follow a blocks manual to the tee? Or did you let your imagination run wild, creating spaceships with wheels and houses that floated? In life, as in blocks, sometimes the most memorable creations come from unexpected combinations. Pursue your unique vision, even if it defies norms.

3. Brick by Brick: Small Steps to a Bigger Picture

You can't just wish a castle into existence. It's built one brick at a time. Similarly, dreams don't materialize overnight. Each effort, each little step, is a brick towards making your vision a reality. Relish in the process.

4. Dealing with Missing Pieces

Ever been in the groove of building, only to find that you're missing a piece? Frustrating, right? But that's when you improvise. In life, we often face obstacles or lack resources, but creativity is about making the best with what you have.

5. When Your Creation Doesn't Stand

Sometimes, what we envisioned doesn't translate well into reality. Your block tower might collapse, and your initial plans might falter. But hey, that's an opportunity to revisit, reimagine, and rebuild. Each version gets better.

Building Thoughts:

Life, dude, is pretty much like that box of blocks. It can be organized and planned, or spontaneous and chaotic. But whatever you choose, let creativity be your guide. Envision, dream big, and remember—each brick, each step, counts. And sometimes, the magic lies not in the final product, but in the joy of creating it. So, here's to building our dreams, one colorful piece at a time!

3:3 Interlocking Pieces: The Value of Connectivity and Community

"Ever tried building a grand blocks tower with just those flat, singular pieces? No? Because it's kinda impossible, right? That's the thing with building blocks... and life. We're designed to connect."

1. Each Brick has a Role

In a structure, every piece, no matter how tiny or seemingly insignificant, plays a role. Similarly, in our communities and social circles, every individual brings something unique to the table. Value isn't just about size or visibility; it's about contribution.

2. Strength in Unity

Two building blocks locked together are tougher to break apart than one alone. There's strength in unity. Wh we face challenges, having a supportive community or a friend to lean on can make all the difference. Together, we stand more robust.

3. Not Every Piece Will Fit... And That's Okay

You know that frustrating moment when you're trying to jam a building block piece where it doesn't quite fit? We experience that in life too. Not every relationship or connection will be seamless, and that's fine. It's about finding where we fit best and valuing those connections.

4. Building Bridges, Not Walls

Blocks teach us that with a little creativity, we can transform barriers into bridges. Life's disagreements or misunderstandings are opportunities to create understanding, empathy, and stronger bonds.

5. Adapting and Evolving Together

As kids (okay, and adults too), our block creations evolve. A house turns into a spaceship, which then becomes a dinosaur. Communities and relationships also evolve. Recognizing, respecting, and adapting to that growth is the essence of lasting connections.

Brick-by-Brick Wisdom:

Imagine if each of us were a building block piece. Unique in color, size, and function. Yet, designed to connect. Life's richness, dude, comes from these interlocking moments. Moments where we find our fit, create something bigger than ourselves, and learn the unparalleled value of togetherness. It's kinda magical how a tiny plastic block can teach us the depth of connectivity and community. So, next time you click two building block pieces together, remember – in unity, there's strength, beauty, and endless possibility.

Chapter 4: Lessons from the Colorful Bricks

"Alright, so building blocks. You'd think they're just toys, right? But man, there's a universe of wisdom in those colorful, interlocking bricks. From the box to the building, there's so much these bricks can teach us about the bigger picture. Explore with me into the rainbow of lessons."

1. Every Color has its Place

Just like the diverse shades of blocks, we encounter countless personalities and experiences in life. Embracing diversity, whether in thought, action, or identity, adds richness to our world, just as different colored bricks make a structure more vibrant.

2. Sometimes, Simplicity Speaks Volumes

Ever noticed how even the simplest of designs can be so captivating? Similarly, in life, it's often the simple moments, gestures, and words that leave the deepest impact. It's a gentle reminder that you don't always have to go big to be significant.

3. The Balance Between Instruction and Intuition

Building block sets come with manuals, guiding us step-by-step. But isn't it thrilling to go off-book sometimes? Life, too, has its norms and expectations. However, the magic often lies in those moments where we trust our gut and take the unconventional route.

4. Overcoming the Pain of Stepping on a Building Block (Literally!)

Stepping on a rogue block is a rite of passage (and, yep, it's agony). Life, like a scattered block floor, is filled with unexpected twists and stumbles. But with each step (and ouch moment), resilience grows.

5. Deconstruction Before Reconstruction

There's a kind of beauty in breaking down a block structure to rebuild something new. Life's like that too. Our plans and dreams may sometimes fall apart, but that often gives way to rebuilding, reimagining, and reinventing ourselves in ways we hadn't thought possible.

Building Block Wisdom:

You see, those plastic bricks aren't just kid stuff. They're little life teachers, each with a lesson or two. From them, we learn about diversity, resilience, creativity, simplicity, and transformation. So, the next time you're holding a handful of colorful building blocks, remember – they're not just toys, they're tokens of timeless truths. Dive into the colors, embrace the play, and let life unfold one brick at a time.

4:1 Patience and Persistence: When Your Creation Falls Apart

"Man, I remember it like it was yesterday. I was deep into building this massive block castle - towers, moats, drawbridges, the works. Just as I was about to place the final brick, the table jolted, and my hours of work crashed down. Heartbreak in a jumble of colorful pieces. But, as I stared at the rubble, I found lessons far beyond just block building."

1. Every Collapse has a Cause

In the moment, it might seem like our efforts spontaneously crumble, but there's always a reason. Maybe it's a shaky foundation, maybe a rushed step. Similarly, life's setbacks, while sudden, can often be traced back to an oversight or miscalculation. Recognizing and understanding these causes helps in rebuilding and prevention.

2. Initial Despair is Natural (and Okay)

When something we're passionate about falls apart, that sinking feeling is inevitable. Whether it's a block tower or a life project, the heartache is real. Embrace the disappointment; it's a testament to your dedication and passion.

3. Rebuilding Can Lead to Reinvention

As I looked at the scattered bricks, I had a choice: recreate the same castle or design something new. Often, our setbacks provide an opportunity to innovate. When life knocks down our efforts, we get the chance to rebuild, often in better, more imaginative ways.

4. Past Mistakes Become Future Precautions

After the castle incident, you can bet I was careful about securing my building blick base and ensuring no sudden jolts. Life's failures and setbacks are lessons in disguise. They arm us with experience, making us wiser and more cautious in our future endeavors.

5. Patience and Persistence are Powers

It would've been easy to give up, to leave the bricks scattered. But the beauty of building (and life) is in patience and persistence. With every rebuilding effort, you reinforce your commitment and passion, proving that setbacks can't diminish your spirit.

Brick by Brick, Step by Step:

Life, like a delicate block creation, has its moments of fragility. There will be times when things seem to crumble, when all seems lost. But remember, each collapse carries lessons, each setback is a setup for a comeback. With patience, persistence, and a pinch of perspective, you can always rebuild, often creating something even more spectacular than before. So, chin up, builder. The world awaits your next masterpiece.

4:2 Following Instructions vs. Going Rogue: Balancing Guidance and Intuition

"Dude, do you remember the first time we opened that huge building block box? The booklet was thicker than my school textbook, and every step meticulously detailed. It felt like a blueprint to creating a masterpiece. But there was also that one summer afternoon, remember? No booklet, no guides, just a wild imagination and a sea of bricks. We built bizarre structures, probably ones that the manufacturer never imagined. Both experiences were fun, in different ways."

1. The Comfort of a Guided Path

There's something comforting about having a clear-cut path, whether it's a building block manual or life's unwritten rulebook. It offers predictability, a sense of knowing that if you follow steps A, B, and C, you'll get a certain result. It's the tried and true, the path most trodden. In life, this might be the 'safe' choices—like studying a conventional subject or taking a stable job.

2. The Thrill of the Unknown

Going rogue with those block pieces was thrilling! We didn't know what we'd end up with, and that was the beauty of it. Similarly, in life, straying off the beaten path, trusting your gut, and following your passions can lead to unexpected and often rewarding outcomes. It's riskier, yes, but the potential for unique experiences and self-discovery is immense.

3. The Value of Blending Both

While it's fun to get lost in freestyle building or life decisions, sometimes, it's the blend of structure and spontaneity that yields the best results. Think about jazz music - a structured base rhythm with moments of wild, unpredictable improvisation. That's the sweet spot! Life's like that too. Sometimes, you follow the rules; other times, you listen to your heart and break a few.

4. Recognizing When to Pivot

As we explored our rogue block adventures, there were times we realized a structure wasn't going as planned. Similarly, in life, when you trust your intuition, it's equally essential to recognize when things aren't working and pivot accordingly. It's about being flexible and adaptable, knowing when to stick to the plan and when to chart a new course.

5. Embracing the Journey Over the Destination

Whether you're meticulously following a guide or going wild with your creativity, it's the process that counts. Building with blocks or living life, the joy is in the journey—the mistakes, the surprises, the eureka moments. The outcome is just the icing on the cake.

To Guide or To Rogue, That's the Question:

Life hands us blueprints, sure. There are guidelines, societal norms, and tried-and-tested methods. But there's also your inner voice, aching for expression, daring you to dream and defy. Balance is key. Know when to follow the manual and when to throw it out the window. In the end, it's about crafting a life that feels right for you, piece by colorful piece.

4:3 The Joy in the Process: Celebrating the Building, Not Just the Finished Product

"Man, I remember when we'd dump all those pieces on the floor, the rainbow cascade of possibilities stretching before us. Initially, we were so focused on what the end design would be—a castle, a spaceship, a mini-city. But soon, we realized something profound. The real magic? It wasn't just holding the finished product; it was in every moment leading up to it."

1. The Beauty of 'Now'

In today's fast-paced world, we're often so goal-oriented, always looking to the future. But there's a unique kind of joy in being present, cherishing every step, every challenge, every little win. Whether building a block masterpiece or building our lives, the 'now' holds experiences that we'll never get back.

2. Mistakes and Learning

When one piece didn't fit or we misplaced a block, it wasn't a setback; it was a lesson. Each 'oops' moment with those building blocks taught us patience, creativity, and resilience. In life too, our missteps aren't failures but stepping stones, shaping us, refining us, making our eventual success sweeter.

3. The Bonds Formed Along the Way

Building wasn't a solitary endeavor. We brainstormed, laughed, debated the color of the next block, and sometimes even squabbled. In the grand scheme of things, it wasn't about the block tower but the memories made, the bonds forged. Similarly, in life, it's the people we journey with, the relationships we nurture, that truly matter.

4. Valuing Progress Over Perfection

Our block designs weren't always perfect. They leaned, they lacked symmetry, but they were uniquely ours. They represented progress, creativity, and hours of dedication. Life's like that. It won't always be picture-perfect, but every step, every effort, is worth celebrating.

5. The Unexpected Surprises

Remember stumbling upon that rare piece we thought we'd lost? Or accidentally creating a design better than we'd imagined? These were the unplanned joys, the serendipitous moments. Life, in all its unpredictability, offers such surprises. It's not just about the big wins but also the unexpected moments of happiness and discovery.

Embracing Each Moment:

We live in a world that glorifies outcomes—the finished product, the end goal. But real richness lies in the journey, the laughter, the tears, the learning, the growth. Whether you're piecing together colorful bricks or charting the course of your life, remember to relish each moment, each challenge, each victory. Because, in the end, it's not just about where you get to, but how you got there.

Chapter 5: Into the Great Outdoors: Camping

"Oh, the allure of the great outdoors—sitting around the campfire, trading stories under the twinkling canvas of the night sky! Camping brings to mind the crackle of the fire, the aroma of toasted marshmallows, and the refreshing chill of the morning dew. There's something raw and authentic about it, taking us back to our roots, and man, the lessons it's laden with!"

1. The Essence of Simplicity:

Camping teaches us the beauty of simplicity. We're stripped down to the basics, away from the buzz of technology and the clutter of possessions. It's about experiencing the world in its raw form, realizing that joy isn't in things, but in moments, in connection, in the rustle of leaves and the murmur of the night.

2. Resilience and Resourcefulness:

When you're out in the wild, it's all about adapting and overcoming. Maybe the wood's damp, or you've forgotten the matches. The situations demand resilience, pushing us to find solutions, to improvise. It's a metaphor for life itself—facing challenges head-on, getting creative, bouncing back stronger.

3. Community and Connection:

Camping binds us. It's huddling together for warmth, sharing stories, cooking over the open flame. It reminds us of our inherent need for connection, for shared experiences. In the digital age, where interaction is often reduced to likes and comments, it reinstates the value of genuine conversation, of truly being with people.

4. Reflection and Introspection:

The tranquility of nature invites introspection. Away from the daily grind, it's a space to reflect, to understand ourselves better. Those silent hours under the stars, the whispers of the wilderness—they spark thoughts, help us align with our deeper selves, and reveal what truly matters.

5. The Inherent Bond with Nature:

Being enveloped by nature, feeling the earth under our feet, witnessing the dance of the fireflies—it awakens a primal connection. It's a reminder of our intertwined existence with the environment, sparking a sense of responsibility and a desire to protect and preserve.

Learning from the Wilderness:

Camping isn't just a getaway; it's a journey brimming with lessons, a gentle teacher whispering the secrets of life. It molds our perspectives, reinforces values, and imprints upon us the importance of connection, adaptability, simplicity, and conservation. So, let's seek the solace of the wilderness, embrace its teachings, and carry its lessons into our daily existence, becoming embodiments of the wisdom the great outdoors graciously offers.

5:1 Preparing for the Journey: The Significance of Planning and Preparedness

Ever been caught in a sudden downpour on a hike? Or arrived at a campsite to realize you forgot the tent stakes? Moments like these aren't just minor inconveniences; they're powerful lessons on the importance of planning and preparedness.

1. The Map Isn't the Territory:

Planning is essential, but it's also crucial to understand that the map we design isn't the actual journey. Life can throw curveballs, and while it's impossible to prepare for every scenario, a solid plan provides a framework, a guiding light.

2. Setting Clear Objectives:

Just as you wouldn't head into the wilderness without a clear destination or purpose, life also requires clarity of intent. Whether it's a personal goal, a career milestone, or a life dream, knowing your 'why' keeps you oriented when the path gets challenging.

3. Gathering Resources:

The best trekkers know the importance of a well-packed backpack. Similarly, in life, assembling the right tools, knowledge, and skills in advance can make the difference between a smooth journey and a tumultuous one.

4. Anticipating Challenges:

Weather changes, path blockages, or wild animals — seasoned adventurers prepare for these. Life's challenges might not be as clear-cut, but anticipating potential obstacles and having contingency plans can save a lot of heartaches.

5. Flexibility in the Plan:

No matter how much you plan, sometimes, things just don't go as expected. Maybe the campsite is full, or a trail is closed. The beauty lies in adapting, in finding a new viewpoint, or a different route to the destination. Preparedness isn't just about sticking to the plan but being ready to change it when needed.

6. Building Confidence:

There's a distinct confidence that comes from knowing you're prepared. It's the assurance that, come what may, you have the resources and the mindset to tackle it. This confidence isn't just for the trails; it's a life skill.

A Step Forward:

In the end, whether you're setting up camp under the stars or charting out life's next big adventure, preparation is more than just a safety net; it's a foundation. It allows us to face the unknown with courage, to navigate challenges with wisdom, and to embrace life's journey with open arms. So, prep up, plan, and then, with confidence and excitement, step into the vast wilderness of possibilities.

2. Adaptability: Rolling with the Punches

Camping is the ultimate test of adaptability. Forgot the can opener? Time to get creative. Fire won't light? Maybe those Doritos can be your secret weapon (seriously, they burn!). It's all about rolling with what nature—and life—throws at you. Just like seasons change and animals migrate or adapt, we too should learn to change our strategies, rethink our approaches, and continue moving forward.

3. Beauty of Simplicity: Less is Often More

One of the coolest things about camping? Realizing you can live with so much less. Suddenly, a simple meal of beans and rice tastes like a feast, and a clear night sky? Beats any movie night. Life's like that. We often get bogged down by the frills, the excesses. But strip it down, and you see what truly matters. Love, laughter, memories—no WiFi necessary.

Parting Wisdom:

Nature is one heck of a teacher. And camping? It's like enrolling in a masterclass on life. Resilience, adaptability, simplicity—these aren't just fancy words. They're the essence of a fulfilling life. So the next time you're out there, surrounded by the whispers of the trees and the melodies of the night, remember: you're not just camping. You're learning the art of living. Cheers to that!

5:2 Campfires and Connections: Valuing Community and Shared Stories

"Man, there's just something about campfires. The crackling of the wood, the dancing flames, and the warmth that brings everyone a bit closer, both physically and emotionally. And let's not forget those marshmallows, slowly roasting to a gooey perfection. But you know what's the real magic? It's the stories. The tales, the memories, the shared laughter, and even the silences that say more than words ever could."

1. The Power of Gathering:

You've felt it, right? That electric energy when people come together. Like how the cold seems a bit more bearable when you're huddled up with your buddies. Campfires remind us that there's strength in numbers. Just as a lone ember might die out quickly, but together, they form a blazing fire, humans too thrive best in the company of others. We aren't meant to go through life solo.

2. Shared Stories: Building Bonds

Remember that time your friend shared that hilarious story about their first camping mishap? Or that touching tale of their childhood? Stories are the threads that weave our lives together. They bridge gaps, foster understanding, and create a tapestry of shared experiences. Through them, we see the universality of human experiences—joys, sorrows, fears, and dreams.

3. The Art of Listening:

A good campfire isn't just about the tales told; it's also about the ears that listen. In this age of constant chatter and digital distractions, truly listening is a lost art. But as the fire crackles and the night deepens, campfires gift us the chance to truly tune in—to the stories, the subtle nuances, the unspoken words, and the heartbeat of the world around us.

4. Reflection and Introspection:

Ever stared into those flames and felt a strange sense of calm? A moment of clarity, perhaps? Campfires, with their warmth and gentle light, create the perfect backdrop for introspection. They allow us to reflect on our journey, our choices, and our dreams.

Parting Wisdom:

So the next time you're sitting by a campfire, marshmallow stick in hand, take a moment. Look around. Cherish the faces illuminated by the firelight, the stories that flow, and the connections that deepen. For in that circle, you're not just sharing warmth and tales, but pieces of your soul. And buddy, that's the stuff life's made of.

Cheers to campfires and the timeless tales they inspire!

Chapter 6: Lessons Under the Stars

"Picture this: Lying on a soft patch of grass, the night air crisp against your skin, and above you, a vast, infinite canopy of twinkling stars. Each one a distant sun, a beacon in the vastness of space. Makes you feel small, doesn't it? But in that insignificance lies a profound lesson about life, purpose, and our place in the grand tapestry of existence."

1. **The Humbling Vastness:**

When you gaze up at the Milky Way, strewn across the night sky, it's hard not to feel a sense of humility. It's a gentle reminder that we are but a small speck in the vast universe. But rather than diminishing our worth, it emphasizes the beauty of our existence amidst such vastness.

2. **Everything is Connected:**

Ever heard of the butterfly effect? One small action can set off a chain of events with far-reaching consequences. Just like stars in constellations, every action, decision, and thought we have is interlinked, creating the story of our lives and impacting those around us.

3. **The Beauty of Constancy and Change:**

While many stars seem eternal, the truth is they too have lifespans. They are born, they live, and they eventually fade away. The night sky teaches us the value of both constancy and change. To cherish the constants in our life, while also embracing the inevitability of change.

4. Dreams and Aspirations:

How many of us, as children or even as adults, have looked up at the stars and made a wish? The stars encourage us to dream, to aspire, and to hope. They're a testament that even in the darkest of nights, there are pinpricks of light to guide and inspire us.

5. The Universe's Rhythms:

The rhythmic dance of celestial bodies—the phases of the moon, the shooting stars, the rise and set of constellations—teaches us about life's rhythms. There are times of brightness and times of darkness, and each phase holds its unique beauty and lessons.

A Stellar Thought:

So, the next time you find yourself under a starlit sky, take a moment. Breathe in the beauty, the silence, and the wisdom the stars offer. Realize that you, too, have the power to shine, to dream, and to make an impact, no matter how big or small. And always remember, in the vast expanse of the universe, you are here, you exist, and you matter. Cheers to the lessons learned under a sky full of stars!

6:1 Navigating Without Technology: Trusting Instincts and Reading the Natural Signs

In a digital age, we're constantly bombarded by pings, notifications, and GPS voices telling us which way to turn. Yet, before satellite guidance and smartphones, humans had been finding their way using nature's signs and their instincts. What might seem ancient or primitive is, in many ways, a lost art of deep connection and trust.

1. Listening to the Inner Compass:

Deep within us, there's an intuitive voice, a gut feeling. While technology offers convenience, it can sometimes drown out this inner compass. By disconnecting from screens, we learn to trust ourselves more and make decisions rooted in instinct.

2. Reading Nature's Clues:

The position of the stars, the direction of the wind, or even the behavior of wildlife can all provide navigational hints. Just as our ancestors once did, learning to interpret these signs helps us feel connected to the world around us, cultivating a sense of belonging and understanding.

3. Embracing Uncertainty:

Without digital aids, there's an element of uncertainty in navigation. This mirrors life where not everything is predictable. By embracing this uncertainty and facing it head-on, we cultivate resilience and adaptability.

4. Valuing the Journey Over the Destination:

When we're not entirely sure where we're headed, we pay more attention to the journey itself. We become more present, noticing the details around us and appreciating the beauty of the moment. It's a reminder that sometimes, life's value lies in the experience, not just the end goal.

5. Lessons in Humility:

Realizing that we don't have all the answers and sometimes need to rely on the natural world or the kindness of strangers for direction instills humility. It's a poignant reminder that we're just a small part of a vast universe.

Finding the Way Forward:

In navigating without technology, we rediscover the age-old wisdom of our ancestors and the world around us. We're reminded of the beauty of simplicity and the power of trust — trust in ourselves, in others, and in the universe. The next time you find yourself lost, literally or metaphorically, pause. Look around, trust your instincts, and find solace in knowing that sometimes the best paths are the unplanned, unexpected ones that we carve for ourselves.

6:2 Minimalism and Resourcefulness: Making Do with What You Have

The modern world often teaches us that more is better. A bigger house, a newer car, a fuller wardrobe. Yet, as the clutter piles up, so does a sense of dissatisfaction. In contrast, there's something freeing, grounding, and profoundly fulfilling about embracing minimalism and resourcefulness.

1. The Beauty of Less:

There's a reason why many are drawn to minimalist aesthetics, be it in art, design, or lifestyle. Minimalism is about distillation — reducing things to their essence. When we strip away the excess, what we're left with often shines brighter, and we're able to see the true value in what we possess.

2. Unburdened Living:

Holding onto too many possessions or commitments can feel like a weight. By letting go, we can breathe easier, think clearer, and move through life with more agility and purpose.

3. Cultivating Creativity:

Being resourceful often requires creativity. When we have fewer resources, we become adept at thinking outside the box, finding multiple uses for a single item, or reimagining how we can fulfill our needs.

4. The Gratitude Shift:

When we focus on making do with what we have, we cultivate a deeper appreciation for those things. A simple meal becomes a feast, and a warm blanket on a chilly evening feels like the ultimate luxury. By reframing our perspective, we find joy in the everyday.

5. Environmental and Financial Benefits:

Minimalism and resourcefulness aren't just personally enriching; they're beneficial for the planet and our wallets. Using fewer resources means a smaller carbon footprint, and spending less on things we don't need translates to financial freedom.

6. Strengthening Resilience:

Life is unpredictable. Embracing minimalism and resourcefulness fortifies us for the times when things don't go as planned. We become adept at handling situations with grace and finding solutions with limited means.

Finding Abundance in Scarcity:

There's a paradox in minimalism and resourcefulness: by having less and making do, we often gain more. More space, more freedom, more clarity, and a deeper sense of contentment. As we navigate our paths, let's remind ourselves that the most fulfilling life isn't about accumulating, but about experiencing, appreciating, and making the most of every moment with just what we have.

6:3 The Quiet Reflection: Insights from Solitude and Disconnection

The modern world is loud. Between the pings of notifications, the constant hum of urban life, and the clamor of daily responsibilities, finding moments of genuine quiet and reflection is increasingly rare. Yet, it's precisely these moments—when we disconnect from the digital din and reconnect with our inner selves—that some of life's most profound insights emerge.

1. **The Sound of Silence:**

It's an odd thing, but when we step away from noise, both literal and figurative, we often "hear" more. In silence, the voice inside us grows clearer. We find space to process thoughts, mull over decisions, and truly listen to our intuition.

2. **Depth Over Breadth:**

In our interconnected world, it's easy to skim the surface of topics, relationships, and even our own emotions. Solitude allows us to dive deep, to explore the intricacies of our minds and souls without distraction.

3. **A Break from Comparison:**

When we disconnect from the online realm, we temporarily free ourselves from the constant comparisons that social media can foster. In solitude, there's no keeping up with the Joneses. There's just you, as you are, in the present moment.

4. Nature as a Guide:

For many, solitude is best experienced in nature. Trees, rivers, and mountains have a timeless wisdom, teaching us about patience, resilience, and the beauty in each phase of existence.

5. Restoring Balance:

It's okay to admit that we sometimes feel overwhelmed. Regular intervals of solitude can act as a reset button, restoring our mental and emotional equilibrium.

6. Recognizing Our Own Company:

There's an old saying: "If you're lonely when you're alone, you're in bad company." Embracing solitude helps us enjoy our own company, ensuring we're not seeking relationships from a place of desperation, but rather genuine connection.

Cherishing the Quiet Moments:

Solitude isn't about isolating ourselves but about nurturing a relationship with our inner being. It's a dance between connecting with the world and retreating to recharge. In these quiet reflections, we find strength, clarity, and a deeper appreciation for the world around us. So, as the world continues its relentless pace, let's not forget the power and insight waiting in those hushed moments of solitude.

Chapter 7: Intersecting Insights

Have you ever noticed how seemingly unrelated experiences can teach us the same fundamental truths about life? A barista's careful attention to making the perfect latte, a musician's dedication to their craft, or a child's persistence in building a blocks tower—each of these, in their own way, can shed light on larger truths about dedication, patience, and passion.

When exploring the worlds of acting, building blocks, and camping, it might appear at first glance that these domains are vastly different. However, when we scratch beneath the surface, intersecting insights emerge, binding these experiences together in a tapestry of life lessons.

1. Mastery Through Repetition:

Whether it's rehearsing lines for a play, constructing a block masterpiece, or setting up a campsite, repetition is the key to mastery. It teaches us patience, resilience, and the value of perseverance.

2. The Role of Imagination:

Actors transport audiences to different worlds. block enthusiasts create universes from plastic bricks. Campers immerse themselves in nature's canvas. Each of these requires imagination—a reminder that no matter the context, our ability to dream and envision is one of our most potent tools.

3. Presence in the Moment:

There's an innate requirement for mindfulness in all three activities. Whether you're lost in a role, engrossed in placing bricks, or sitting by a campfire under a starry sky, being fully present enriches the experience immeasurably.

4. The Power of Community:

Whether it's the camaraderie among cast members, the shared excitement among builders, or the bond formed between fellow campers, these activities highlight the significance of community. They teach us that while individual effort is vital, it's the collective energy that amplifies success and joy.

5. Embracing Failure as Part of Growth:

Mistakes are a natural part of any endeavor. A forgotten line on stage, a misplaced building block, or a tent that won't pitch—each setback, no matter how trivial or significant, offers a lesson. They remind us that failure isn't the opposite of success, but rather a stepping stone towards it.

Uniting Threads:

It's fascinating to observe how life, in its infinite complexity, offers us repeated lessons across various platforms. The beauty lies not just in recognizing these intersecting insights but in applying them universally. So, the next time you find yourself in a seemingly unique situation, pause and reflect. There might just be a familiar lesson staring back at you, waiting to be acknowledged and embraced.

7:1 Where Acting, Building Blocks, and Camping Collide: Overlapping Lessons from Diverse Experiences

At a cursory glance, acting, building blocks, and camping might appear as disparate experiences, each with its distinct realm and ethos. However, when one delves deeper into the essence of these activities, a beautiful synchronicity emerges. The stage, the playroom, and the wilderness are more intertwined than we initially perceive, revealing lessons that are remarkably universal.

1. Crafting a Vision:

Whether it's visualizing a character's emotional arc, imagining a sprawling block metropolis, or picturing a serene camping site by a lakeside, each endeavor begins with a vision. These experiences underscore the importance of having a clear goal, reminding us that every grand achievement begins with a dream.

2. The Nuances of Problem-Solving:

An actor might grapple with the challenge of portraying a complex emotion, just as a building block enthusiast might ponder over integrating a tricky piece. Meanwhile, in the wilderness, one might need to find a way to set up shelter amidst unforeseen weather conditions. Each scenario, unique in its essence, reinforces the age-old wisdom: Life doesn't present problems without solutions; it's all about perspective and perseverance.

3. Collaboration is Gold:

The theater thrives on the synergy of its ensemble, much like a building block project often becomes more splendid with collaborative creativity. Camping, too, becomes a joyous affair when there's shared laughter and combined efforts in gathering firewood or cooking a meal. These activities echo the profound truth that while individual brilliance is commendable, collective effort often paves the path to unforgettable experiences.

4. Embracing the Journey:

Whether it's the rehearsals leading up to the final act, the joy of assembling bricks, or the trek to reach the perfect camping spot—it's often the process that's more enriching than the endpoint. Life, in its entirety, is an ongoing journey, and the moments of growth, struggle, joy, and discovery are what make it truly vibrant.

5. Resilience in the Face of Setbacks:

A flubbed line on stage, a block structure crashing down, or a camping mishap like forgotten equipment—all teach us the invaluable lesson of bouncing back. They serve as gentle reminders that it's okay to fall, as long as we gather the courage to rise and venture forth once more.

The Confluence:

While acting, building blocks, and camping each offer a realm of unique experiences, their overlapping lessons are testimonies to life's universal truths. They teach us about vision, problem-solving, collaboration, the beauty of the journey, and the undying spirit of resilience. So, the next time you find yourself on stage, with a box of colorful bricks, or amidst the embrace of nature, remember: the wisdom you gain transcends the confines of that moment, seeping into the broader tapestry of life's grand play.

7:2 Building Your Life's Script: Drawing from Play, Creativity, and Adventure

"Life is not a dress rehearsal," they say. But what if we could infuse the spontaneity of a play, the inventiveness of blocks, and the daring of camping into the grand narrative of our existence? Just imagine how rich our life's script could be!

1. The Prologue - Embrace Childhood Curiosity:

Remember those days when we'd don costumes and enact elaborate fantasies in our backyards? Or hours spent creating whimsical block worlds? This uninhibited imagination is where our life's script begins. It's a gentle reminder that our initial approach to life was always rooted in curiosity, wonder, and boundless creativity.

2. Setting the Scene – Choose Your Backdrop:

Just as a camper selects a site or an actor chooses a stage, we have the power to select the environment that best fosters our growth. Whether it's surrounding ourselves with uplifting individuals or actively choosing positivity, the setting we create plays a pivotal role in our life's narrative.

3. Drafting Characters – Valuing Relationships:

An actor thrives on chemistry with fellow performers. Similarly, the essence of our life's script hinges on the relationships we nurture.

Like the interlocking pieces of blocks, each individual we bond with adds depth, color, and structure to our storyline.

4. Plot Twists – The Power of Adaptability:

The unpredictability of a camping trip, the thrill of improvisation on stage, or the sudden collapse of a block tower – life, too, is replete with unexpected turns. It's our ability to adapt, to re-script our narrative, and find alternate paths that truly defines our journey.

5. The Climax – Revel in Life's Peaks:

Those moments of standing ovations, gazing at a completed blocks masterpiece, or witnessing a breathtaking sunrise on a camping morning – these are the crescendos of our life. They are fleeting, yet profoundly impactful, reminding us to cherish our accomplishments, no matter how big or small.

6. Epilogue – Lessons from the Journey:

Every play concludes, every structure is eventually disassembled, and every camping trip concludes with a return home. However, it's the memories, experiences, and lessons learned that linger. Our life's script, too, is less about the destination and more about the richness of the journey.

Curtain Call:

As the curtain falls on our life's stage, it's essential to recognize that we are the playwrights, directors, and protagonists of our narrative.

Drawing inspiration from play, creativity, and adventure allows us to craft a tale that is not only uniquely ours but also one that resonates with vibrancy, depth, and authenticity. So, grab your pen, unleash your imagination, and remember: life is the grandest play you'll ever star in. Make it a blockbuster!

7:3 Ensemble Cast: The People Who Shape Our Lives' Narrative

"Man, I've had such a day, you wouldn't believe it," Jake mumbled to his best friend, Ben, while nursing a steaming mug of coffee at their favorite local café.

Ben smirked, "Try me."

"That's the thing, buddy," Jake sighed, "It's not about one event. It's about everyone. From the taxi driver who shared his immigration story, to my co-worker Sarah who's battling cancer with such grace, to the young barista here who's juggling night school. They're all so... I don't know... pivotal?"

Ben leaned in, "What you're seeing, mate, is the ensemble cast of your life. It's not a solo act, you know."

Life, much like a meticulously directed stage play, is rarely a one-man show. Behind every riveting performance lies an ensemble cast - the unsung heroes who might not always be in the limelight but are integral to the plot. Let's explore deeper into understanding the role of these key players:

1. The Lead Roles - Core Relationships:

These are the ones we turn to at the end of a challenging day - our family, closest friends, or even pets. Their impact is direct, palpable, and forms the essence of our daily lives.

2. The Supporting Characters - Teachers, Mentors, Colleagues:
Much like the scaffolding that gives structure to a building, these individuals provide guidance, support, and often act as sounding boards. Their influence, though sometimes understated, plays a pivotal role in shaping our choices and perspectives.

3. The Extras - Strangers and Acquaintances:
The barista who remembers your daily order, the security guard who always smiles, or the random stranger who offered an umbrella on a rainy day. Their fleeting appearances in our lives often bring unexpected joy, lessons, or insights.

4. The Cameos - Inspirational Figures:
These could be historical figures, authors, celebrities, or any individuals we might never meet but who influence us deeply through their life stories, achievements, and legacies.

5. Behind-The-Scenes Crew - Unsung Heroes:
Think about the garbage collector, the mail carrier, the farmer, or even parents doing unseen sacrifices. Their roles might not be overtly evident, but their contributions are indispensable to the smooth progression of our narrative.

In The Spotlight:

While we are undeniably the protagonists of our stories, it's essential to recognize and value the myriad characters that enrich our plot. They challenge us, support us, teach us, and most importantly, they add depth and color to our narrative.

Jake finally responded, a knowing smile playing on his lips, "You're right, Ben. Every person truly adds a scene, a chapter, or even just a line to our story. But without them, the story wouldn't be half as compelling."

Ben raised his mug, "Here's to our ensemble cast!"

Chapter 8: Application in Daily Life

The bell rang, signaling the end of yet another monotonous school day. As the hallways filled with students eager to head home, Mark found himself reflecting. In the midst of cramming for exams, preparing for basketball tryouts, and navigating the ever-complex social ecosystem of high school, where did his childhood joy and creativity vanish?

But Mark was determined. He realized that to make his daily life more vibrant and fulfilling, he needed to apply some out-of-the-box thinking. Here's what he learned:

1. **The Classroom Isn't Just for Textbooks:**

While Physics might not be everyone's cup of tea, Mark discovered that by visualizing himself as part of the scenarios — be it a spaceship or a pendulum — he not only grasped the concepts better but also made the lessons more engaging.

2. **Morning Routines with a Splash of Fun:**

Mark turned his alarm song into his current favorite track. Waking up became less of a chore and more of a private concert!

3. **Homework Hacks:**

Instead of the usual silent study, Mark and his friends started 'study jams.' They'd pick a subject, collaborate on notes, and teach each other. Mark found he remembered things better when his buddy explained it using a crazy analogy.

4. Fitness Beyond the Gym:

Rather than the usual treadmill run, Mark made it a point to play basketball with friends or skateboard in the park. It wasn't just about physical fitness, but also about relishing the outdoors and sharing laughs.

5. Conversations Over Texts:

While texting was quick and easy, Mark realized real conversations were becoming rare. He made it a point to call a friend or chat face-to-face, finding depth and connection in these interactions.

6. Weekend Recharge:

Weekends weren't just about parties or movies. Mark began exploring hobbies - from photography to cooking. It was about rediscovering passions and finding new ones.

7. Digital Detox Hours:

Mark chose an hour every day where he'd stay away from his phone and laptop. Be it reading, meditating, or simply laying on the grass and staring at the sky, it was his way of reconnecting with himself.

"You know," Mark said one day as he painted a canvas in the art room, "Life's what you make of it. And I choose to paint mine with as many colors as possible."

High school life, with its rigors and challenges, may seem daunting. But Mark's perspective teaches us that every day offers a chance to infuse creativity and joy. It's about finding balance, cherishing little moments, and, above all, making conscious choices to live fully.

8:1 Strategies to Embrace Play and Creativity in Routine

"Man, remember the days when we'd just grab a stick and it would turn into a sword, and the backyard was our vast battleground?" Jason mused, reclining on the school lawn with his buddies. High school had brought new challenges: homework, exams, sports practice, and that ever-present pressure to "figure things out". Amidst it all, that innocent, unbridled creativity seemed like a distant memory.

Yet, deep within, that imaginative spirit still flickered, and here are some ways Jason found to reignite it amidst his high school hustle:

1. Doodle in the Margins:

Yeah, that math lecture might be dragging on, but who says those notebook margins need to be boring? Jason often sketched superheroes or random scenes, keeping his creative juices flowing.

2. Music & Movement:

Those five minutes between classes? Perfect time to pop in earbuds and let loose with some air guitar or drumming on the locker. Jason's friends often joined in, turning it into a mini jam session.

3. Lunchtime Challenges:

Jason and his friends turned lunchtime into a challenge. Some days, it was about crafting the most bizarre sandwich concoction. Other times, they'd make up short, impromptu stories or skits.

4. Gaming with a Twist:

Video games are great, but Jason loved adding his own rules. Maybe it's doing voice-overs for the characters or playing with self-imposed handicaps – it made routine gaming nights way more entertaining.

5. Weekend DIYs:

Instead of binge-watching shows, Jason started diving into DIY projects. From customizing his skateboard to building weird gadgets, it was all about creating something cool from scratch.

6. Story Swap:

For English class assignments, Jason and his friends started swapping their stories for fun, adding their own twists and turns. It turned the usual homework grind into a whirlwind of wild tales.

7. Sports with a Spin:

Basketball was Jason's game. But who says you can't mix things up? Playing in costumes, or creating wacky rules, like 'left-hand shots only', added a whole new level of fun.

"You know," Jason said, as he shot a paper ball into the trash can, envisioning it as the game-winning three-pointer, "we might be growing up, but that doesn't mean we can't keep playing. It's just about finding new ways to make things fun."

Growing up might seem like an endless treadmill of expectations and responsibilities. But as Jason realized, there's always room for play and creativity. It's just about seeing the world through a lens of fun, and sometimes, challenging the routine.

8:2 Finding Your Stage, Building Blocks, and Wilderness in Everyday Settings

The high school cafeteria buzzed with its usual energy, but today, Alex felt different. As he sat there, sandwich in hand, he began to imagine the cafeteria as his stage, his classmates as his audience, and the surroundings as props. Suddenly, lunchtime turned into a performance, where Alex was both a spectator and a star.

Drawing from his drama classes, his childhood love for building blocks, and the camping trips with his dad, Alex started viewing the world around him in a new light. Here's how he wove these

Exercises and Practices Inspired by Acting, Building Blocks, and Camping

As Kyle sat in his room, surrounded by a mix of theater scripts, scattered building block pieces, and camping gear, he couldn't help but see the connections among the three. Eager to share his revelations with his peers, Kyle jotted down some exercises and practices inspired by his diverse passions:

1. Role Reversal:

Inspired by Acting

Every week, try stepping into someone else's shoes. Spend a day understanding a classmate's routine, their challenges, and strengths.

This helps in fostering empathy, understanding different perspectives, and enhancing social skills.

2. The Blocks Challenge:

Inspired by Building Blocks

Using just 50 colorful bricks, create something new every day. It could be a small structure, a random design, or a replica of something you saw. This boosts creativity, problem-solving, and the realization that even with limited resources, possibilities are endless.

3. Nature's Detox Hour:

Inspired by Camping

Spend an hour each week unplugged, outdoors. It could be the backyard, a nearby park, or just a walk around the block. This is a great way to reconnect with nature, de-stress, and recharge.

4. Character Monologues:

Inspired by Acting

Choose a character from a book, movie, or even someone you know. Write and perform a 2-minute monologue from their perspective. This encourages creative writing, deepens understanding of character development, and strengthens self-expression.

5. Memory Building Blocks:

Inspired by Blocks

At the end of each month, choose significant moments and represent them using building blocks, creating a visual diary. This serves as a reflection tool and a way to value small achievements and challenges overcome.

6. Camp Out At Home:

Inspired by Camping

Turn your living room or bedroom into a campsite for a night. Use blankets as tents, make s'mores in the oven, and share stories. This is a fun way to relive camping experiences and bond with family.

7. Improv Games:

Inspired by Acting

Gather a group of friends and play improvisation games. Not only are these hilarious and entertaining, but they also sharpen quick thinking and adaptability.

8. Building Block Journaling:

Inspired by Blocks

Instead of writing, convey your day or feelings using building blocks structures. It's a unique way of expressing without words, focusing on colors, shapes, and forms.

9. Morning Nature Mindfulness:

Inspired by Camping

Start your day with a 5-minute mindfulness exercise, taking

inspiration from nature sounds. It sets a positive and calm tone for the rest of the day.

Kyle shared these exercises with his school's hobby club, and they were an instant hit! They realized that blending different passions could lead to such diverse and enriching experiences. Through these exercises, Kyle and his peers discovered the joy of intertwining their interests and the life lessons each brought along.

Conclusion: Life's Ongoing Lessons

"Dude, high school's wild," Max remarked, leaning against his locker and adjusting the straps of his backpack. The metal doors of the school echoed with the din of teenagers, each busy with their own thoughts, dreams, and heartbreaks.

"Man, you're telling me," replied Jake, rolling his eyes. "One moment you're acing your math test, and the next, you're tripping in front of your crush. Life's like, 'Gotcha!' all the time."

Max chuckled, "Oh, don't remind me of the crush drama! But seriously, every day feels like a lesson, right? Like, yesterday, I learned that sometimes, no matter how much you rehearse, things don't always go as planned."

Jake tilted his head, "Oh, the play rehearsal? I heard about the set crashing down."

Max nodded, "Yeah, but it wasn't just about the set. It was more... symbolic, you know? I mean, you can prepare and plan, but life will still throw curveballs. And sometimes, all you can do is improvise."

Jake grinned, "Speaking of improvising, remember our camping trip last summer? We forgot the tent poles and had to sleep under the stars. Best mistake ever!"

Max laughed, "Absolutely! It's like life was teaching us to find joy in the unexpected. Or like when we tried building that massive block tower, and it kept falling apart? We learned that sometimes, you need a solid foundation before reaching for the skies."

"And that it's okay to rebuild and start over," added Jake.

Both boys paused for a moment, taking in the weight of their words. High school wasn't just about grades or making the team; it was a microcosm of the larger world. A place where they faced rejection, embraced victories, learned about friendship, and confronted their fears.

Max sighed, "You know, it's funny. Adults always tell us that school days are the best days of our lives. But they never say it's also where some of our toughest lessons come from."

Jake nodded, "True. But we also learn resilience. We learn to bounce back, to keep pushing, and to believe in ourselves. And the best part? We're learning together."

Max smiled, "Couldn't have put it better. Here's to more lessons, more memories, and growing up together."

As the bell rang, signaling the end of the day, the two friends walked side by side, knowing that while school was temporary, the lessons they were learning would last a lifetime.

Embracing New Teachers: Finding Wisdom in Unexpected Places

Jay and Benny sat on the bleachers, watching the sun cast long shadows across the soccer field. They had been buddies since elementary school, navigating the labyrinth of adolescence side by side. Today, they were talking about the unusual places they had found wisdom.

"You know, man," Jay began, fidgeting with his shoelaces, "I always thought wisdom came from textbooks, or maybe those profound quotes teachers put up on classroom walls."

Benny laughed, "Or from grandpas with long beards in movies, telling tales of their youthful days."

Jay chuckled. "Exactly! But lately, I've been realizing that sometimes the best lessons don't come from where we expect."

Benny raised an eyebrow, curious. "Oh? Do tell."

Jay sighed, looking out at the field. "Like Mrs. Thompson. She's just the janitor, right? But the other day, I saw her patching up a torn soccer net with such care. I asked her why, and she said, 'Every stitch keeps the dream alive for someone.' It hit me hard, dude. Here she was, finding purpose and imparting wisdom in what many consider a mundane job."

Benny nodded, impressed. "Wow. That's deep."

"And there's more," Jay continued. "Remember that stray cat behind the cafeteria? I've started feeding it, and you won't believe the patience it's taught me. That wary little thing took weeks to trust me. It made me realize trust isn't a given; it's earned."

Benny grinned. "Man, even a cat's your teacher now?"

Jay laughed, "Seems so! And don't get me started on video games. They've taught me strategy, patience, and even a bit about history. Assassin's Creed, anyone?"

Benny snorted, "History might be a stretch, but I get your point."

Jay leaned back, "Life's got funny ways, man. It's like the world's a classroom, and everyone and everything's a potential teacher. We just gotta be open to the lessons."

Benny thought for a moment. "So, you're saying we should be open to learning, not just in class but from every experience?"

"Exactly," Jay affirmed. "And from everyone, regardless of their title or status. Everyone's got a story, a lesson. We just need to listen."

The two boys sat in reflective silence, the setting sun painting the sky in shades of gold and crimson. High school was just a chapter, and they were only beginning to grasp the vastness of the world's curriculum. But with open minds and hearts, they were ready to embrace the unexpected teachers that life would undoubtedly present.

The Invitation: Seek, Learn, and Grow from All of Life's Experiences

nnor's phone buzzed beside his homework-filled desk. Another notification, another distraction. He picked it up to find a text from his older cousin, Alex: "Ever tried journaling? Helped me a lot during my high school days. It's an invitation to learn from life." Connor squinted. Journaling? Sounded more like a chore than a cool pastime. But out of respect (and slight curiosity), he responded: "How does it work?"

Alex's reply came swift: "It's simple. At the end of each day, write down one thing you learned or observed. Big or small. It's all about seeking insights and growing from them."

Though skeptical, Connor figured he'd give it a shot. That evening, with nothing but a pen and a notebook, he scribbled down a thought about a conversation he'd overheard between teachers. The days that followed saw notes about a skateboard trick gone wrong, understanding a friend's perspective, and even the phases of the moon.

Two months later, that journal became a mosaic of experiences, challenges, and revelations.

One evening, while flipping through the pages, Connor's younger brother, Max, peeked over. "What's that?"

"It's a journal. An...invitation of sorts," Connor replied.

Max raised an eyebrow, intrigued. "Invitation to what?"

"To seek, learn, and grow from everything, dude. Even from that time you accidentally dyed the cat green."

Both brothers burst into laughter, but amidst the humor, a realization dawned. Every event, every challenge, every ordinary day was an invitation to learn. To see the world not just as a series of unrelated events, but as a rich tapestry of experiences that had so much to teach.

By the end of the school year, Connor's journal was brimming. But more importantly, his perspective had shifted. High school wasn't just about textbooks and tests. It was about learning from every interaction, every failure, every victory.

And as graduation neared, with the vast expanse of life awaiting, Connor felt prepared. For he had learned to accept life's constant invitation: to seek, to learn, and to grow. Not just in big, profound moments, but in the quiet, seemingly mundane ones too. Because, as he'd discovered, wisdom often lurked in the most unexpected places.

Parting Thoughts: Your Personal Journey and What Lies Ahead

The final bell rang, echoing in the vast corridors of Westwood High. Jake stood there, his locker emptied, his yearbook filled with scribbles and memories, his heart a mix of nostalgia and excitement. High school. Man, what a ride!

He remembered walking into the building as a freshman, sneakers squeaking, heart pounding, wondering how he'd ever find his way. Now, as a senior, he was leaving with more than just an academic education. He had life lessons, ones no textbook could teach.

Jake leaned against the locker and thought about those early days. The desperate need to fit in, to be part of the popular crowd, to ace every test. And then came the realization - he didn't need to be part of a crowd; he needed to find his crowd. Those who appreciated his love for graphic novels, his secret talent of juggling, and his passion for stargazing.

High school had been about understanding that the path isn't always straight. Like that time he tried out for the basketball team but didn't make the cut. Heartbroken, he stumbled upon the drama club and discovered a love for acting. He learned that sometimes, detours lead to beautiful destinations.

He remembered late-night cramming for exams, the pressure, the stress. But also the joy when the drama team won the state competition. The pride when he helped paint the school mural. The happiness when he finally understood algebra (thanks to Mr. Lawson's relentless patience). High school had shown him that there are many ways to define success.

But what lay ahead? College, work, a thousand unknowns. Yet, Jake wasn't afraid. He had learned resilience, the power of perseverance, and the importance of community. He knew that every end was a new beginning.

Gazing around the now-empty hallway, Jake felt gratitude. High school had given him not just knowledge but wisdom. He had discovered that everyone is on a unique journey. There's no set roadmap, no predefined destiny. We craft our stories, making them as adventurous, as exciting, or as simple as we wish.

Closing his locker for the last time, Jake whispered a silent thank-you to Westwood High. For the lessons, the memories, and the friendships. As he stepped out into the sun, his heart was light, ready for the next chapter.

Because life, with all its ups and downs, was an adventure. And Jake? He was just getting started.

Afterword

As I prepare to write this afterword, I find myself reflecting not just as a reader, but as a Stepfather who has had the privilege of watching a young man grow, learn, and carve out his own unique path. "Freedom & Responsibility: What I Learned About Life from Acting, Building Blocks, and Camping" is more than just a collection of experiences. To me, it is a testament to the resilience, passion, and unyielding spirit of my Stepson. It's a firsthand glimpse into his world, where every challenge became an opportunity and every experience a lesson learned.

I recall the countless times he'd come home with tales from his acting classes, the passion in his eyes evident. I remember the countless hours spent building with him, each piece a symbol of patience and vision. There were the numerous camping trips - where nature became both a playground and a teacher, teaching him the essence of responsibility.

Being a Stepfather has its own set of challenges. You step into a world already in motion, hoping to find your place in it. In this journey, I've learned as much from him as he might have learned from me. His quest for the Eagle Scout rank wasn't just his journey; in many ways, it became ours. Through every high and low, the bond we've built and the mutual respect we've cultivated is something I cherish deeply.

Watching Joseph finish this book, I feel a mix of pride, gratitude, and awe. It goes without saying that it's an impressive feat, in and of itself, to start and finish the creation of your own book. Such an incredible achievement and milestone for any aspiring author. Moreover, to see someone you care for deeply navigate life with such maturity and perspective is truly a gift. I've told my Stepson on many occasions that I would definitely want to be lifelong adult friends with him if I didn't already have a Stepfather/Stepson relationship. He is the type of person whom you want to have in your life in any capacity. With all that being said, I hope that as you've turned each page, you've not only seen the heart of a young Eagle Scout but also felt the universal threads that bind all of us in this intricate dance of life.

      To my Stepson: Your journey has been incredible to witness, and I'm honored to have been a part of it. To every reader: May you find inspiration in these pages and recognize the beautiful dance of freedom and responsibility in your own life.

With immense pride and love,

Dr. Aaron Drew

Dr. Aaron Drew

Appendices

Books:

"The Perks of Being a Wallflower" by Stephen Chbosky
- A coming-of-age story that captures the highs and lows of adolescence. A must-read for anyone navigating high school.

"Mastery" by Robert Greene
- For those interested in mastering a skill or hobby, Greene breaks down the path to becoming a master in any field.

"Into the Wild" by Jon Krakauer
- An adventurous tale that resonates with anyone feeling the call of the wild or yearning for a break from conventional life.

Workshops:

Acting Classes at the Local Community Center
- Enter into the world of acting and understand character development, improvisation, and more.

Building Blocks Robotics Workshop
- Take your block building skills to the next level. Collaborate, design, and program your creations.

Survival Skills Camp
- Experience the great outdoors, learn about campfires, navigation, and basic survival techniques.

Experiences:

Local Theater Performances
- Support community theaters and get inspired by local talent.

Stargazing Nights at the Observatory
- Understand the vastness of the universe and maybe even spot a constellation or two!

Weekend Camping Trips with Friends
- Disconnect from technology and reconnect with nature.

Interactive Activities and Challenges for Readers

Character Role Swap
- Spend a day as someone else. Maybe a character from your favorite book or movie. Observe how people interact with you.

Building Block Blueprint Challenge
- Without any instructions, create a unique colorful block structure. Share it with friends or family and see who can replicate it fastest.

Nature's Scavenger Hunt
- On your next walk or camping trip, make a list of things to find or observe in nature.

Feedback Circle
- With a group of friends, share one positive trait and one area of improvement for each other. Take it in good spirit and use the feedback for personal growth.

Digital Detox Day
- Spend 24 hours without any gadgets. Observe the change in your mood, attention span, and interactions.

Build Your World
- Using building blocks (or any other building material), create a model of your ideal world. Share it with others and explain the significance of each element.

Night Under the Stars
- Spend a night outside – in your backyard or a safe open space. Reflect on your thoughts, jot down your feelings, or just enjoy the serenity.